Original title:
Shadow of the Sycamore

Copyright © 2025 Creative Arts Management OÜ
All rights reserved.

Author: Aidan Marlowe
ISBN HARDBACK: 978-1-80566-815-2
ISBN PAPERBACK: 978-1-80566-814-5

Beneath the Arbor's Embrace

Squirrels debate, who's the best at hide,
Hiding their treasures and giggling with pride.
A cat takes a nap, in this leafy retreat,
While ants hold a march, on parade for the feast.

Birds chirp loudly, they think they can sing,
While below, the grasshoppers hop with a fling.
A dog rolls around, trying to fit in,
This humor in nature is where all begins.

The Dance of Leaves in Twilight

Leaves twist and twirl in a whimsical glow,
They mimic the dancers who put on a show.
The breeze plays a tune, only they can hear,
As crickets provide the orchestra's cheer.

Fairies sneak out when the sun starts to yawn,
They laugh at the moon, who's still wearing his dawn.
The wind tickles noses; oh, what a delight,
As the stars join the party, twinkling so bright.

Shade Beneath the Embrace

In the cool of the green, a picnic is spread,
With sandwiches stolen, and juice boxes bled.
Kids play tag with the shadows, it's quite a scene,
While dogs chase their tails in a game unforeseen.

A frog tries to leap but lands in a snack,
While everyone giggles, as he wiggles back.
The ants hold their meeting, debating a plan,
To steal a crumb worthy of a banquet's span.

Stories Woven in Branches

Each branch has a tale; just listen, it's true,
Of raccoons and owls, and one wily shrew.
They gather at dusk, swapping gossip and dreams,
In a world full of laughter, or so it seems.

The wind whispers secrets as the daylight runs,
While ladybugs chime in, they're hardly done.
They share silly riddles till the night draws near,
In the boughs of the tree, we all laugh and cheer.

Stories Weaved in Green

In leafy tales where laughter grows,
A squirrel wears shoes that nobody knows.
With acorns stacked high, a market fair,
While birds take bets on a tumble through air.

The rabbits debate the best kind of hat,
A floppy old thing or one sleek and flat.
With tumbleweeds dancing in the breeze,
They argue and fuss, then just laugh with ease.

The Veil of Verdant Dreams

A raccoon holds court by the old garden gate,
With daisies his throne, he can hardly wait.
He tells wild tales of long-ago nights,
While passersby giggle at his quirky sights.

The frogs all croak out a choir of glee,
As they leap for the stars, oh so gracefully.
They plan a grand ball in a puddle so wide,
With lily pad floats and a water bug slide.

Murmurs of the Woodland Soul

In chuckling burbles of the brook's soft flow,
A gnome juggles mushrooms, putting on a show.
The trees whisper jokes in a raucous delight,
While fireflies dance on a cool summer night.

Chattering chipmunks play tag by the creek,
While a tortoise decides he's the one who'll sneak.
He moves at a pace that's slower than slow,
Yet somehow he wins! Oh, the tortoise's show!

In the Half-Light of Eternity

Under the boughs where the giggles echo,
A hedgehog in bow tie gives quite the cameo.
With spines all a-glimmer, he twirls in the sun,
A dance full of wobble—oh, he thinks it's fun!

The owls roll their eyes at his clumsy display,
Yet join in the jig as they hoot in their play.
With twinkling stars casting spells from the skies,
The forest's a stage for their comical tries.

Beneath the Wide Embrace

Under broad branches, we play and gleam,
Squirrels scamper, a lively team.
A picnic basket, crumbs all around,
Ants march in line, a tiny sound.

Laughter echoes in dappled light,
We dodge the squirrels, oh what a sight!
A rogue chipmunk steals a sandwich, oh dear,
His tiny victory brings us good cheer.

Memories Etched in Bark

Carvings and hearts, a lover's delight,
Grinning faces, in the soft twilight.
The bark may be rough, but memories stay,
A timeless currency, come what may.

From picnics tossed on breezy days,
To squirrel chases in silly plays.
Each scrape and notch—a story told,
Laughter like leaves, unfurling bold.

The Chorus of Hidden Life

Bees humming tunes in a buzzing spree,
A dance of colors, funny as can be.
Crickets chirping just to compete,
A symphony layered under our feet.

The rustle of leaves, a squirrel's reply,
To a joke only birds can imply.
The woodpecker drums in comedic rhyme,
Nature's giggles, a timeless mime.

Reflections in the Leafy Caress

In the gentle sway, peppers peek through,
Tomatoes giggle in the morning dew.
A breeze whispers secrets, funny and bright,
As grasshoppers leap, a joyful sight.

Each leaf a mirror of things to adore,
With every sway, there's laughter in store.
Under the sun, laughter flows free,
A whimsical dance, just nature and me.

Shadows in Stillness

In the garden, squirrels plot,
Chasing dreams they might have caught.
A bird's squawk ignites the chase,
While ants march in a silly race.

Old leaves dance with a playful breeze,
Twisting, turning with such ease.
The cat napping lies in deep thought,
Regarding every strange, funny spot.

Beneath the tree, a shadow creeps,
Wonders what the sly fox keeps.
A laugh erupts from branches tall,
As a hat falls, oh what a sprawl!

Even the sun can't hold a grin,
As wily winds invite a spin.
Nature's comedy unfolds its lore,
Amidst the laughter, we all want more!

Flickers of Life in Green

A frog leaps with a joyful note,
While beetles take a tiny boat.
The grasshoppers join in the show,
With dance moves we'll never know.

Crickets chirp a rhythm divine,
As fireflies blink and intertwine.
The smell of pie wafts through the air,
What kind of magic could be there?

A bee, with swagger, floats on by,
Hums a tune with a friendly sigh.
While blooms giggle, shades of bright,
With petals fluttering in delight.

Branches sway in a puppet play,
Catching giggles in the light of day.
Nature's theater, staged just right,
Will keep us grinning all through the night!

The Enchanted Undertow

Inking whispers through the leaves,
A prankster breeze, oh how it weaves.
Mice canoodle, near the creek,
Sharing secrets with a cheeky squeak.

The water tickles tiny toes,
As fish wiggle in fancy clothes.
A gopher peeks, then back he dives,
Swapping tales of wild lives.

Leafy hats are all the rage,
Rabbits hop with a silly stage.
Each splash holds a quirky jest,
In this world, laughter's truly blessed.

Nature smiles, a jest to share,
With quirky antics everywhere.
Join the frolic, embrace the play,
As whimsy rules the sunny day!

The Embrace of Wood and Sky

Between the limbs, a bird's delight,
Spins its tales from morning light.
Butterflies pull pranks on bees,
As nature giggles in the breeze.

Acorns drop with a comic thud,
As chipmunks dance in a playful flood.
The trunks stand still, as if in awe,
Of every jest that they saw.

A playful wind shakes the tree,
Rustling leaves, tickling glee.
Each ripple creates a jolly wave,
In this nook, mischief is brave.

Under this dome of wood and sky,
Laughter echoes, oh my, oh my!
Let's dance along to the nature's song,
In a world where humor truly belongs!

Soft Footfalls on Forest Floors

With every step, a crackle sounds,
A symphony of twigs beneath my bounds.
I tiptoe past the squirrels high,
Who judge my grace with a winked eye.

The mushrooms giggle, dressed in spots,
Encouraging me to tie my knots.
I trip on roots and make a fuss,
As nature laughs; oh, how they cuss!

The leaves are dancing, they tease me so,
Whispering secrets where wild laughter flows.
In this lively wood, I'm quite the clown,
Sporting my twig crown like a jester's gown.

As I prance and pirouette with flair,
Even the deer can't help but stare.
Life is a waltz upon the ground,
Where every stumble comes laughter's sound.

A Symphony of Nature's Echo

Birds chirp loudly, but one sings flat,
The frogs join in, with a ribbit splat.
A raccoon joins, with a bang and a crash,
Making music from all sorts of trash.

The wind plays notes through leafy highs,
Tickling the branches, a sly surprise.
A squirrel conducts, with acorn baton,
Leading our concert until the dawn.

The rabbits hop, in a syncopated dance,
While beavers try to perfect their prance.
Nature's orchestra, in this sweet glade,
Who knew the forest held such a parade?

With every beat, my heart skips a bounce,
As the flowers sway and all creatures flounce.
Together we laugh, our sounds intertwined,
In this enchanting melody, pure and unconfined.

The Heartbeat of the Elder Grove

In the woods, where the old trees peek,
Echoes of laughter in the leaves, they speak.
A wooden bench squeaks, painted in glee,
As I settle down for a chat with a bee.

The ancient bark whispers tales of yore,
Of giggling fairies that danced on the shore.
Mossy giants chuckle, their secrets they share,
Each ring in their trunks holds a bit of flair.

I fumble my jokes, in this grand reverie,
But the owls hoot back in totality.
As the sneaky raccoons lift sweets from my pack,
I smile and wave; they won't get it back!

In this lively grove, where time takes a seat,
Every heartbeat's a rhythm, every moment's a treat.
I'll spin my stories, impress the tall trees,
In the company of nature, I do as I please.

Memories Swaying in the Breeze

The willow whispers, saying, 'What's that?'
As a cheeky cat prances, chasing her hat.
Sunflowers giggle and sway in the sun,
While ants march in rhythm, oh what fun!

The breeze swirls tales of a jumping frog,
Who leapt for a fly, and then got stuck in a bog.
I laugh at the thought, with a wink and a tease,
Wondering if he'll ever find his ease.

Butterflies flutter, putting on a show,
Painting the air with colors that glow.
Each wave of the breeze carries chuckles anew,
As memories dance, both old and askew.

In this playful realm, where laughter can please,
Every moment's a treasure, tossed by the breeze.
Let's create a story, full of giggles and cheer,
Where nature and whimsy forever endear.

Secrets in the Leaves

In the tree, leaves giggle, they hide,
A secret world where squirrels confide.
Acorns are treasure, the prize of a jest,
While friendly birds debate who's the best.

When wind tickles branches, laughter erupts,
As chipmunks declare they're the leaf-munching pups.
In this leafy realm, the fun never ends,
Nature's comedians, laughter transcends.

Dancing on breezes, with stories to share,
Eccentric whispers float through the air.
Nature's own stage plays a lighthearted part,
In the canopy's embrace, joy's always an art.

So listen closely, dear friend, take heed,
In this leafy laughter, there's always a need.
For secrets are silly, and silliness sweet,
In the whimsical life of the grove's heartbeat.

The Shadekeepers' Lament

Beneath the wide trunk, a guardian sighs,
The critters are plotting their next big surprise.
With shadows that dance and giggles that bloom,
The shadowy keepers give way to the zoom.

In the night's laughter, the owls make a bet,
Who's scaring more critters? The dog or the cat?
Amidst the fun pranks, the shadows conspire,
A chorus of chuckles, their hearts full of fire.

Yet with every giggle, a sigh starts to form,
The squirrels are slacking, no acorns to swarm.
They're busy with games, in the moonlight they prance,
While the keepers just whisper, waiting their chance.

Oh, shadows that linger, keep spirits in cheer,
In the game of the night, they whisper, "Come near!"
For when fun is afoot, and giggles resound,
Even the shadows can't keep from the ground.

Tales of the Whispering Tree

Once a gnarled tree spun tales at dusk,
Of a raccoon who dreamed of a shiny gold tusk.
The stories flew high on the breeze like a kite,
Whispering humor till the stars shone bright.

A wise old owl with spectacles round,
Critiqued all the tales, such wisdom profound.
"Why do squirrels dance when there's acorn galore?
Prance with your treasures, they laugh and explore!"

With every chirp and rustle of leaves,
The laughter erupts, like winter reprieves.
Each tale told anew, under moon's gentle glow,
Gives roots a sweet giggle, and branches a show.

So gather around, let the whispers commence,
For tales from the tree make perfect sense.
In the heart of the grove, where mischief's the core,
Every leaf holds a chuckle, who could ask for more?

Echoes Beneath the Boughs

Under the boughs, where shadows do play,
Echoes of laughter blend night into day.
The bugs have their parties, the crickets propose,
A dance of the night where everyone knows.

With twirling fireflies tracing each step,
The frogs croak their rhythm, a joyful concept.
In the cool of the dusk, they chirp with delight,
Making melodies sweet, igniting the night.

Just then a raccoon, with a hat made of leaves,
Declared himself king, much to everyone's heaves.
"Let's feast on the berries, and sing songs so loud,
While owls keep watch, wrapped snug in a cloud!"

Beneath boughs that whisper, the woods come alive,
Where every soft rustle gives humor a drive.
In echoes that linger, and laughter that rings,
The night becomes brighter, as joy brightly sings.

Seasons Beneath the Canopy

In spring, the squirrels dance with joy,
Chasing each other, like a flung toy.
Leaves whisper secrets, so verdant and bright,
While ants on a mission march out in the light.

Summer brings picnics, a blanket set wide,
With ants stealing cookies, oh what a ride!
Children play tag, no cares left to cling,
Asblooming flowers pull out their bling.

Autumn leaves fall, golden and bold,
While squirrels hoard nuts, or so I'm told.
People wear sweaters, feeling so fine,
Sharing hot cocoa, with marshmallows divine.

Winter creeps in, with a chill in the air,
Kids build a snowman, with debonair flair.
In this lush grove, a circus unfolds,
Nature's own jesters, breaking the molds.

The Light That Flickered

In a glade where the critters do scamper and play,
A flickering lantern marks night from the day.
Fireflies frequent, in fashion so bright,
While owls do their gossip, in the moonlight.

The chase of a rabbit, the hoot of an owl,
A raccoon pops up, looking quite foul.
With a splash of moonbeams, the stage is all set,
For wildlife shenanigans—what a duet!

A cat naps nearby, with dreams quite absurd,
Of being a lion, the king of the herd.
But as dawn approaches, they start to unwind,
For a sunbeam is beckoning, oh so unkind.

Yet the laughter survives, beneath all the trees,
With the sun filtering through leaves like a tease.
In this whacky play, all creatures unite,
A raucous of life, oh what a delight!

Paintings in the Dappled Sun

Brush strokes of green, splashed with some gold,
Nature's own canvas, a sight to behold.
Dappled sunlight winks through branches so fine,
Creating a stage where all creatures dine.

The rabbits wear coats of ambrosial hues,
While chipmunks hoard stashes of colorful foods.
A parade of insects, oh what a display,
In the masterpiece gallery, come see their ballet.

The deer prance around, like stars on a stage,
In a ballet of nature, free from the cage.
As birds chirp along, with a melodic spin,
And butterflies flutter, with giggles within.

So come one, come all, to this vibrant fair,
Where laughter and colors fill up the air.
In the dance 'neath the leaves, joy cannot be tamed,
For nature's own laughter can never be blamed.

Veils of Time in Green

Through verdant veils, the past likes to peek,
With whispers of laughter, at fun times we seek.
The breeze carries tales of all creatures around,
While mischief abounds, in jokes that we've found.

The hours glide by, like a squirrel on a spree,
Tick-tock, tick-tock, who holds time's decree?
A lizard in shades gives a knowing stare,
While shadows of giggles are scattered everywhere.

Moments are precious, wrapped neatly in green,
With giggles of critters in all that we glean.
A tapestry woven of joy and delight,
Where the dance of the wild keeps the heart feeling light.

So relish the echoes that time has contrived,
In forests of laughter, where wonder's alive.
With every leaf rustle, absurd tales revive,
As smiles shoot forth like a stream in full drive.

In the Gloom of Ancient Branches

Old branches creak, a laugh to tease,
Squirrels dance, as if to please.
A wise owl hoots, in silly tones,
While rabbits jest on their little thrones.

In thickets deep, where whispers grow,
A raccoon slips, with a cheeky show.
The moonlight winks, a playful glint,
As shadows play, they laugh and stint.

The crickets sing, a tune so grand,
They've formed a band, a quirky stand.
The rustling leaves, a giggling sound,
Echoes of joy in the night abound.

Beneath the stars, the antics fly,
With every rustle, a new sly cry.
In this ancient dance, we join the spree,
Where laughter reigns, wild and free.

Secrets of the Silent Grove

In a grove where whispers weave,
The secrets hide, you won't believe.
A fox in boots, a hat askew,
Cracks jokes with birds, a merry crew.

The groundhog grins, he checks the news,
With squirrels glancing at his shoes.
A bag of seeds, he spills with pride,
As chipmunks giggle, running wide.

A rocking chair on branches sways,
While fireflies dance in bright displays.
The shadows chuckle, oh what a sight,
As night unfolds, with pure delight.

Underneath a moon so round,
The joy of mischief knows no bound.
Each cranny hides a tale untold,
In this grove, where laughter's bold.

The Lullaby of Rustling Leaves

Leaves rustle softly, a sweet refrain,
They giggle and chatter, bring joy once again.
The wind tells secrets, a mischievous breeze,
As frogs in the pond croak jokes with tease.

A hedgehog hums, with a twinkling eye,
His spiky coat, oh my, oh my!
He treads with care on the leaf-strewn floor,
While critters roll 'round, begging for more.

The moonlight twinkles like giggling stars,
As rabbits bounce in their tiny cars.
They race through the grass, a silly parade,
In this haven of fun, where laughter's displayed.

With each gentle shiver of branches tall,
The trees share tales, we're all in thrall.
Their lullaby stirs, in this playful night,
Where giggles and whispers take playful flight.

Dreams in the Dappled Shade

In patches of sunlight, dreams abound,
Where whispers mix with laughter sound.
A turtle juggles, what a sight,
While ladybugs cheer, with all their might.

A butterfly flutters, wearing a crown,
She twirls and spins, the envy of town.
With each little flop and flurry, we see,
Nature's own antics, wild and free.

The ants in a line, marching in tune,
Trade stories of crumbs as they commune.
With every presumed, peculiar quest,
They chuckle along, a humorous jest.

Beneath the dance of the leaves so bright,
Dreams make mischief, all through the night.
In dappled shade where laughter is king,
The silliness reigns in the songs we sing.

A Reverent Touch of Nature

In the park, a squirrel twirls,
Stealing acorns, doing swirls.
A bird on a branch plans a surprise,
As it fluffs its feathers, oh how it flies!

The grass is green, the daisies shout,
While ants form lines, a tiny route.
A dog runs by, its tail like a kite,
Chasing its dreams in pure delight!

The Sigh of the Woodland

Woodpeckers rap in a quirky beat,
While rabbits dance on their little feet.
A breeze comes gently, whispers a joke,
As a big mushroom laughs, 'I'm no croak!'

The pine trees sway with silly grace,
Dancing macarena in this wooded place.
While the sun giggles, tucked behind leaves,
Nature's funny games are what it weaves!

Where Light Meets the Dark

Fireflies blink, like tiny stars,
While frogs croak tunes, with no guitars.
In a moonlit dance, shadows pirouette,
A raccoon shimmies, as it's not done yet!

Bats gossip up high in squeaky tones,
While owls hoot truth in clever drones.
It's a nighttime circus, wild and free,
In the land of the weird, come and see!

Mosaics of the Forest Floor

Leaves crunch softly like a sweet treat,
While mushrooms pop up to take a seat.
A snail moves slow with a shell so proud,
Waving to critters, standing out in the crowd!

The ground is a canvas, colors ablaze,
Where nature paints silly, wild displays.
A lizard grins, basking in the sun,
Nature's fun party has just begun!

A Sanctuary Beneath the Branches

Squirrels plan their heist with glee,
Nuts are scattered, wild and free.
They chortle in a comic chase,
As leaves applaud their nutty race.

The branches bend with laughter's song,
Where creatures dance all day long.
A rabbit joins, a grand debut,
With every hop, he steals the view.

A frog jumps in, a leafy king,
With croaks that make the branches swing.
Each critter, part of nature's play,
In this green room, they laugh all day.

Underneath the dappled light,
Life's a joke, and oh, what a sight!
The sanctuary, full of cheer,
In this leafy realm, there's nothing to fear.

Music of the Meadow Floor

Grasshoppers strum their stringless tunes,
While ants march on in comical prunes.
Beetles click in time with delight,
As butterflies join in the light.

The daisies dance with silly flair,
While bumblebees buzz without a care.
A tune of whispers fills the air,
With winks and nudges everywhere.

Amidst the blooms, a dog does prance,
Chasing shadows in a merry dance.
The frogs join in with ribbiting cheer,
Creating a symphony, oh so clear!

Together they form a jolly band,
In this meadow, life is just grand.
With laughter in every petal's sway,
The music of the earth's cabaret.

The Quiet Weaving of Time

Twigs and leaves weave tales of old,
With intricate patterns, stories told.
Time drips slowly like melting ice,
In the stillness, there's humor so nice.

A turtle plots its slow parade,
While a hare zooms off, slightly delayed.
As time unfurls with a clumsy twist,
They share a grin that can't be missed.

A clever fox, with cunning flair,
Tricks a bird who lands unaware.
As giggles echo through the grove,
It's laughter and folly, the sweetest trove.

The sun dips low, the day concludes,
In every pause, a laugh eludes.
As night weaves in with gentle rhyme,
There's joy in the quiet weaving of time.

Whispers of the Forest Heart

The trees huddle close, sharing secrets bright,
Gossip flows between branches in flight.
With rustling leaves that giggle and tease,
In the cool breeze, it's laughter that frees.

A raccoon dons a mask, oh so sly,
With a stash of berries, he's living high.
He winks at a mouse, who can't help but grin,
In the forest's jest, everyone wins!

Woodpeckers drum a silly beat,
As squirrels spin tales while dancing on feet.
Every nook holds a pun, a jest,
In nature's comedy, oh, how we're blessed!

Twilight falls with a chuckle and cheer,
Whispers of mirth linger ever near.
In the forest's heart, joy is the art,
Where humor resides and takes every part.

Requiem of Fallen Leaves

Once green and vibrant, now they cheer,
Their dance in the wind, oh so sheer.
They tumble and twirl in their leafy spree,
As squirrels below shout, "Look at me!"

A leaf complained, "I fell too soon!"
The others giggled, "You missed the moon!"
With acorns laughing, they formed a band,
With every flop, they feel so grand.

The wind plays tricks, like an old prankster,
Leaves yelp, "Help us! We're caught in a flanker!"
Yet on this ground, they giggle and tease,
"Next year we'll fly, just wait for the breeze!"

In piles they're gathered, in heaps they fall,
Their rustling laughter becomes a call.
Though the season may claim their bright attire,
They'll still enjoy life, never to tire.

Guardian of the Forgotten Path

In the heart of the woods, a path laid bare,
Guarded by critters with unexpected flair.
A rabbit stands watch, with a monocle tight,
Dressed in old leaves, oh what a sight!

A hedgehog grumbles, "This trail's a bore,"
While squirrels debate, who could explore.
The oak trees chuckle, sharing their tales,
Of knobbly gnomes and their wild fails.

Each step resonates with a whoopee cushion,
Nature's own prank keeps the path all plushin'.
"Watch your feet!" a wise owl hoots from a tree,
"Or you might trip on a joke, just like me!"

At dusk they gather, the beasts in glee,
Sharing old stories, embracing the spree.
With every giggle beneath the moon's glow,
They guard the path, where the funny winds blow.

The Lullaby of Rustling Leaves

When night falls softly, a rustle begins,
Leaves sing sweet lullabies, dancing on winds.
They whisper secrets, oh so sly,
"Did you hear what the branches awry?"

The moon eavesdrops, giggling on high,
As chirping crickets begin to cry.
With every breeze, the tales unwind,
Of mushrooms who waltzed, rather unrefined.

"Are we falling? Oh, isn't it neat?"
They chuckle and snicker, in rhythmic beat.
In dreams they leap, like jesters of yore,
Twirling and swirling, then falling once more.

Tomorrow they'll cover the ground in cheer,
With patches of laughter throughout the year.
The rustling leaves know how to tease,
With a melody of fun, they dance with ease.

Where the Wildflowers Dream

In a meadow of dreams, wildflowers sway,
With petals that chatter, they giggle and play.
"I'm the prettiest! No, look at me!"
They fight for a glance, a flower decree.

Dandelions tease, "We spread everywhere!"
While tulips blush, cutting the air.
Each bloom has its story, each hue has a quirk,
The daisies debate, who's done the best work.

Their roots intertwine like a funky old dance,
Twisting and turning, they're caught in a trance.
"Let's bloom to the rhythm, let's sway in a spin,"
The breeze joins the fun, with a cheeky grin.

So gather 'round, in the soft morning light,
Where wildflowers dream, and the world feels right.
In the laughter of petals, joy will abound,
Where the sunflowers nod, their smiles profound.

Silhouettes at Dusk

As the sun dips down low,
Silly shapes start to grow.
A squirrel wears a top hat,
While the raccoon's all about that!

The shadows dance with glee,
Jumping high on a nearby tree.
A rabbit sporting shades of cool,
Makes the evening feel like a school!

With each twist and turn they make,
A line of ducks begins to shake.
Oh, what fun in the fading light,
They leap and hop, a comical sight!

In this playful twilight,
All the fuss seems just right.
Nature's jests under the moon,
Each laughter blooms, a playful tune!

A Tapestry in Green

In a field where plants are plump,
A frog's decided on a jump.
Geese are painting the grass blue,
With splashes of laughter, they brew!

Leaves rustle like a giant hand,
Tickling all across the land.
Butterflies adorn their wings,
Joining in on all the flings!

A hedgehog rolls down a hill,
Collecting laughs — what a thrill!
While gophers throw their hats in cheers,
Mixing joy with shouts and jeers!

And as fireflies flash their glow,
The night unfolds its funny show.
In this green and jolly scene,
Life's a jest, so bright and keen!

Reverie in the Thick of It

Underneath branches so wide,
Squirrels have a picnic side by side.
With acorns served on tiny plates,
They laugh and dance while stealing mates!

A porcupine juggles little nuts,
While the owls hoot, "What's the fuss?"
They sing songs of the silliest kind,
In a grove where joy is intertwined!

A lizard struts in shiny shoes,
Announcing the latest dance moves.
All the critters gather near,
To cheer for the star with happy cheer!

In that tangle where laughter grows,
Even the shyest critter knows.
To join the fun, just slip right in,
'Cause under branches? Let the games begin!

Beneath the Broadening Horizon

The sun spills gold like melted cheese,
Critters cheer, dancing in the breeze.
A hedgehog wiggles with pride,
While a fox surfs down the tide!

A dance party starts on the grassy floor,
With all the animals wanting more.
Bunnies bounce like they're in a trance,
One knits while leading the dance!

Chasing shadows, it feels so light,
As butterflies twirl in sheer delight.
Every critter's got a best friend,
As laughter echoes with no end!

Beneath the big sky's laughing face,
Nature's jesters win the race.
In this land, so vast and bright,
Life's a comedy — what a sight!

The Veil of Memory Leaves

In the park where laughter sways,
A squirrel steals an old man's gaze.
He drops his ice cream on the grass,
And giggles echo as it splats.

Beneath the tree, a dog takes flight,
Chasing shadows in pure delight.
A cat yawns wide, with an airs' glance,
While birds discuss the latest dance.

A picnic blanket on the floor,
Holds a sandwich, but—what's that for?
The ants throw a feast they can't outrun,
While kids just chase the setting sun.

So lend an ear to nature's play,
Where silly antics rule the day.
Each giggle wraps a memory tight,
As laughter echoes into the night.

Beneath the Serpent's Tongue

A snake in shades, so cool and sly,
Winks at birds that just float by.
In this tall grass, secrets abide,
Where mischief's always set to ride.

The lizards laugh at the sun's hot beam,
They sip cool drinks, it's quite a dream.
A frog wears shades, is feeling slick,
He tells a joke, and man, it's quick!

Tails entwined in a tango of fun,
Reptiles dance, while bugs will run.
Underneath the laughter and yawn,
Mischief waits for the early dawn.

So if you wander where the scales gleam,
Remember, life is more than it seems.
With every chuckle, they'll give you a grin,
Join in their joy, and let the fun begin!

The Wilderness Chronicle

In a forest dense, a bear decides,
To wear a hat and go for rides.
He steals fine honey, but look! A bee,
Buzzing with rage, his hat's not free!

A raccoon, sly, with a clever grin,
Gathers trash bins, that's where the win.
While deer start planning a runway show,
With fir and leaves as their grand tableau.

A chatty bird claims the highest perch,
Declaring the wildest gossip search.
While squirrels toll at the garden gate,
Announcing it's time for late-night fate.

So come, my friend, to the woods so wild,
Where critters dance, and chaos is styled.
A tale unfolds behind each tree,
Of funny escapades, wild and free!

Voices Among the Outliers

A shy tree leans, it starts to sway,
Listening in on what the bushes say.
With giggles caught in a breeze's trek,
They scheme of plans, oh, who's a wreck?

The mushrooms gossip over sunshine's spill,
While squirrels play tag, over the hill.
A flower turns, pink with delight,
As whispers flutter, a silly flight.

Underneath each leaf, laughter grows,
While shadows chuckle, who really knows?
The world's a stage for critters' frolic,
Making the mundane seem quite symbolic.

Join the ruckus, let your worries fly,
In this leafy realm, every sigh is a pie.
So lift your spirits, be part of the sound,
Among the outliers, pure joy is found!

In the Stillness of Green

Under branches so wide, birds do sing,
A squirrel dances, thinking it's king.
The grass tickles toes, a giggle escapes,
As nature wears laughter in leafy shapes.

A bug with a hat crawls right on by,
Making a fuss as it tries to fly.
With every step on the cushy ground,
A symphony of giggles is all around.

A rabbit hops, steals carrots in sight,
While chips in the trees cheer a funny fight.
The sun winks down with a wink of a grin,
Nature's beloved comedic spin.

Amidst the green, oh what a scene,
Where laughter and whispers twirl like a dream.
In this stillness of cheer, let us play,
For every little moment is a funny ballet.

Chronicles of the Verdant Veil

In a forest where frogs start a band,
With moss as their stage, it's all quite grand.
They croak out a tune, 'neath branches so low,
As rabbits debate if they should join the show.

A deer with a bow tie prances about,
While owls hoot softly, trying to shout.
The trees are aghast at such antics near,
As nature's great circus unfolds with cheer.

With every rustle, a secret slips out,
A hedgehog recites, his voice full of doubt.
What's next on the list for this woodland tale?
Perhaps a dance-off, or a funny derail?

So gather around, let laughter unite,
Among the lush greens, all feel just right.
The chronicles weave with a giggling spin,
As nature invites the fun to begin!

Twilight's Gentle Caress

When dusk draws near, the fireflies blink,
They play little games, or so we think.
A raccoon in glasses sips from a cup,
While crickets play chess, and never look up.

The moon grins wide, wearing shades of delight,
As stars trot out for their twinkling night fight.
With whispers of mischief and sparkles of grace,
Nature giggles softly, embracing the space.

Chasing shadows, the fox does a flip,
While giggles erupt from the owl's funny quip.
In this nightly ballet of playful jest,
There's joy in the stillness, a whimsical quest.

And here in the twilight, with laughter galore,
The woods become magic, forever to explore.
So let's dance with shadows, and sing with the breeze,
For twilight's a party among the tall trees.

Embracing the Twilight Glade

In the glade where the giggles grow,
Frogs play hopscotch, their jumps all aglow.
Fireflies flicker, a light-hearted dance,
While raccoons plan pranks to take a chance.

The trees rustle softly, sharing a laugh,
A squirrel enacts a hilarious half.
The flowers all chuckle, swaying in tune,
As the moon peeks in, thinking it's June.

Wandering through this whimsical land,
A fox plays a lute, with style so grand.
The laughter that floats on the breeze like a song,
In the twilight glade, where all things belong.

So join in the mirth, take a seat on the grass,
Where nature's sweet humor is always a blast.
In this playful embrace, let your heart race,
For laughter is magic in this lively place.

The Hidden Stories of Light and Dark

In a grove where giggles blend,
A squirrel tells tales, a furry friend.
Light dances among the leaves high,
While shadows plot with a sly eye.

Sunbeams chase the ants in stride,
While whispers in the gloom abide.
Bugs wear hats and dance in line,
In this place where the moon will dine.

The old wise tree cracks a joke,
As laughter rises like a smoke.
A toad in a crown hops about,
Declaring dusk just a fun bout.

With every breeze, a chuckle grows,
Tickling branches, the silliness flows.
This world of light, full of delight,
Beneath the boughs, there's pure insight.

Beneath the Canopy's Whisper

A porcupine with a flair for mime,
Graffiti in bark, a leafy rhyme.
Underneath the playful sun,
The chatter of nature has just begun.

Pigeons wear shades, cool as can be,
While frogs give thumbs-up from the tree.
Leaves rustle secrets, sweet and amusing,
A chatty chipmunk with tales so confusing.

The ants throw a party, cake made of crumbs,
While beetles drum on fallen hums.
In the lilt of night, the creatures convene,
For jests that only the trees can glean.

Light glimmers down, laughter unfurls,
As fun unravels in whirly swirls.
This is a place, not just timber and barks,
Filled with the giggles of nature's larks.

The Age of the Ancient Watcher

Rusty roots tell a tale of old,
Of mischief and laughter worth their weight in gold.
The wise old trunk grins wide with glee,
As the critters come forth, wild and free.

A raccoon dons a monocle for style,
With critters who swarm, it's a cheeky isle.
Each branch a stage, for antics unplanned,
In this arboreal Netflix so grand.

Fireflies sparkle like sequins at night,
While the owls hoot jokes, a comedic sight.
Past and present weave hand in hand,
In a world where whimsy and wildness stand.

With whispers that swirl 'round the green grand,
The trees shake with laughter, a jovial band.
From roots to crowns, the stories embark,
In the age of a watcher, a light-hearted spark.

Beneath the Solace of Starlight

At dusk, the branches begin their song,
Although in daylight, they are generally wrong.
A cricket's serenade brings the moon near,
The best kind of eco-friendly cheer!

Beneath the stars, the night claims the day,
And fireflies dance, with nothing to say.
The owl spreads wisdom, a pun or two,
While the hedgehogs giggle at the view.

The raccoons host a midnight feast,
With snacks so tasty, they think the least.
A twinkle above, a chuckle below,
As the cosmos joins in on the show.

In the cool night breeze, stories unfold,
Where fun and whimsy are forever bold.
A celestial jester in the vast dark,
Crafting magic, here in the park.

Whispers Beneath the Canopy

Leaves giggle and sway, oh what a sight,
Squirrels are plotting their next big heist.
Branches wave wildly, guiding the flight,
While birds sing the tunes of a fine luau feast.

Mice wear tuxedos, all dressed for the show,
A raccoon's the DJ, he's spinning all night.
Laughter erupts from the roots down below,
As fireflies dance in a twinkly light.

Bumblebees whisper all secrets they know,
Jokes about flowers and silly leaf fights.
The wind tells a story, and we can't say no,
To the tales of the tree that bring pure delight.

Under this laughter, life feels so grand,
With nature's own humor unfolding in sight.
So gather around, lend a humorous hand,
And enjoy every moment, it's all pure delight.

Echoes in the Dappled Light

In the dappled dance where the sun's rays play,
A shadowy group starts to frolic and twirl.
Chattering critters in a mischievous way,
The whispers of mischief make leaves softly swirl.

A toad in a top hat, oh what a grand scene,
While beetles in bowties perform their fine acts.
The dance floor's alive; it's a pure green routine,
As frogs leap like dancers with flair and with cracks.

Pine cones are clapping, their excitement at stake,
The laughter erupts with a flurry of cheer.
You'd think they'd be serious — oh, what a fake!
In this light-hearted grove, it's all about cheer.

So sway with the wildflowers, twirl in delight,
Embrace every giggle that comes from the trees.
For in this bright realm where the sunshine is bright,
There's joy in the frolics, as all laughter frees.

Gnarled Roots and Sunlit Dreams

Under the old tree with roots all a-tangle,
Sit creatures who plot with a gleam in their eyes.
A rabbit in spectacles, she starts to wrangle,
While foxes weave tales with some marvelous lies.

The ants form a band, with sticks as their drums,
And badgers provide all the vocal delights.
Mice dance in circles, while giggling low hums,
In the glimmering rays of the soft morning lights.

Adventures abound in this gnarled old stage,
Where worms write the scripts that produce their reprieves.
Silly ideas? They're the world at this age,
In the playground of nature, there's laughter in leaves.

So come join the fun in this woodland of schemes,
Where dreams come alive in the sunlight so warm.
With every new riddle, each giggle redeems,
The essence of joy in its playful charm.

Secrets of the Elder Tree

Oh, secrets they hide in this ancient old soul,
Branches that gossip with raindrops of sass.
A parrot named Fred thinks he's on a roll,
As he imitates frogs with his colorful class.

Beneath the big branches, a critter's parade,
Tiny feet pitter-patter, quite mischief-filled cheer.
They skip and they hop in a wild charade,
Sharing giggles and whispers for all to hear.

Mice wear capes – oh my, what a sight!
It's a super-hero show full of laughter and glee.
While ants in their regalia march left and right,
In this comical world where they all love to be.

So gather around near the trunk that is wise,
In the kingdom of nonsense where merriment gleams.
For the laughter of nature is one such surprise,
In the joyful embrace of old mystical dreams.

Threads of Time in Tranquil Shade

In the shade, old patterns lie,
Laughter echoes as birds fly high.
Time ticks slowly, but we take a break,
Underneath leaves that gently shake.

The sun sneaks in through a leafy seam,
Where squirrels plot and children dream.
Every giggle has a tale to tell,
In this cool haven where stories dwell.

The Old Tree's Silent Soliloquy.

Oh, tree so wise with tales to share,
You've seen the years, which we declare.
With flapping hats and shoes askew,
You chuckle softly, as if you knew.

Birds in your limbs play tunes so sweet,
While ants march by on their tiny feet.
You stand so tall, with branches wide,
A funny friend on this leafy ride.

Beneath the Canopy's Whisper

Whispers swirl in a musty breeze,
Gossiping leaves tease with such ease.
The bumblebees buzz a tiny tune,
While we share secrets under the moon.

With giggles bouncing off barky trunks,
And mischievous squirrels doing their stunts.
The world slows down for jokes to unfold,
As laughter weaves through the branches bold.

The Dance of Dappled Light

Little patches of sunlight play,
Dancing wildly throughout the day.
While shadows stretch like cats on a rug,
We giggle and dodge, feeling snug.

Each flicker a wink from nature's eye,
As butterflies flit with a graceful sigh.
In this vibrant disco of green and gold,
We twirl through laughter as stories are told.

The Gentle Harbinger

In the park where leaves do dance,
A squirrel wears a tiny pants.
He struts around, a furry chap,
Without a care, he takes a nap.

The birds chirp tunes of silly glee,
While butterflies sip from their tea.
The earth chuckles, it seems to know,
Life's just a play, a grand old show.

The sun winks down, a playful tease,
As ants march off with crumbs and cheese.
A ladybug dons her polka dots,
While grasshoppers jump and tie their knots.

So here we laugh, under the sun,
Life's a jest, let's have some fun.
With critters prancing, all in line,
In nature's fab, comedic shrine.

An Acolyte of the Earth

Beneath the tree where giggles bloom,
A frog in trousers claims the room.
He hosts a dance, a slimy ball,
Where snails are guests and crickets call.

With petals bright, they twine and weave,
Rehearsing lines that none believe.
The earth spins tales of mishaps grand,
Of bees that buzz with no command.

The worms compose a slinky tune,
As fireflies glow beneath the moon.
In mud and muck, they make their art,
With laughter shared, it warms the heart.

And while the daisies sway in time,
The beetle learns to dance and rhyme.
Together wrapped in nature's mirth,
They celebrate this silly earth.

When the Wind Speaks

A gusty whisper floats on by,
It tickles trees, oh my, oh my!
The branches laugh, a rustling cheer,
They gossip tales the critters hear.

The dandelions nod in jest,
As winter's chill begins its quest.
They shed their seeds like confetti bright,
And scatter giggles in flighty flight.

The breeze teases the squirrel's stash,
While pumpkins roll with a comical dash.
"Oh wind," they sigh, "let's play some more,
Bring stories to us—open the door!"

As whispers dance from tree to tree,
Nature joins in, wild and free.
In this caper, oh so grand,
The world is painted with a playful hand.

Illuminations in Twilight

As dusk descends, the fireflies spark,
Little lanterns in the dark.
They flicker ideas, twinkling bright,
And lead the way through the cooling night.

The owls hoot out their wise old jokes,
While crickets strum, and laughter provokes.
A shadow prances, bold and spry,
With mischief swirling, oh my, oh my!

The moon beams down with a wink so sly,
"Tell me your secrets, I'll never lie!"
And frogs croon tunes of moonlit glee,
In the magical realm, you and me.

So as the stars begin to sing,
Here's to the joy that twilight brings.
With every chuckle, a story unfolds,
In the night's embrace, our laughter molds.

Patches of Daydream

In a park where the squirrels play,
A napkin floated like a ballet.
Picnics and laughter filled the air,
While ants plotted schemes with flair.

A sandwich flew, on its quest to roam,
Chased by a raccoon, far from home.
Cake crumbs raining down like confetti,
Nature's party turns wild and sweaty.

The sunlight winks through leafy screens,
As daisies dance in playful scenes.
Beneath the branches, the laughter hums,
While bees hold court with their buzzing drums.

So here we drift in bright daydreams sweet,
Where every snack becomes a treat.
With nature's quirks, we all agree,
Life's great comedy, just you and me.

Secrets Held in Wisps

The wind whispers secrets, oh what a tease,
Telling tales of gumdrops and mischievous bees.
It tickles the leaves with stories so bold,
Of warty toads wearing crowns made of gold.

Clouds chuckle softly, a fluffy parade,
As mismatched socks dance in the glade.
What a mystery spins with the breeze,
A rumor of dancing, bees giggling with ease.

In this forest, the laughter can swell,
Like a chorus of frogs singing quite well.
They leap in a jig on the soft mossy floor,
While crickets compose a giggly encore.

So hold tight your secrets, dear trees and lakes,
Let's laugh with the wind at the joy that it makes.
For in whimsical whispers, we find our delight,
A playful parade through the day and the night.

Lamentations of the Lost Grove

In a grove where the trees wear spectacles tight,
They murmur complaints under moon's gentle light.
"We're losing our leaves! Oh, what a disgrace!"
While the owls laugh softly, enjoying the space.

The pine needles grumble, their needles so pointy,
While tree trunks discuss if their bark's too jaunty.
"Are we trending?" they ponder, "or just standing around?"
As the rabbits break forth with a leap and a bound.

A woodpecker thumps with a rhythm so loud,
Saying, "Don't fret, folks, let's make our heads proud!"
Roots dive for gossip, burrowing low,
While the grass giggles at the tree's funny show.

So let's join the trees in their playful debate,
As they moan about aging, yet dance with such fate.
In this grove of misfits and laughter that flows,
The hilarity blossoms where nobody knows.

Conversations with the Wind

The wind has a style, a breezy old shrouda,
And tickles the tulips with whispers of loud-a.
It chats with the daisies, plotting a jest,
While spinning about like a playful guest.

"Hey there, old oak, have you seen the new sprout?"
It chortles and rumbles, with a giggling shout.
The branches sway gently to join in the fun,
As sunlight winks on, a bright, golden run.

The rush of soft breezes brings hops of delight,
While butterflies flutter, their colors so bright.
"Tell me, dear leaf, do you dance with your friends?"
And leaves rustle back, "Only fun never ends!"

So here in this chat with the soft, frolicsome air,
We find out that friendship's a breath, like an affair.
With laughter and mirth bouncing all around,
Conversations are gold where the giggles abound.

In the Embrace of Wood and Root

Beneath the bark, the squirrels play,
Chasing each other in a daring display.
A raccoon stares, with pie on his face,
Wondering how he got into this race.

The woodpecker drums on a branch so bold,
While a wise old owl watches, or so I'm told.
The trees just laugh as the antics arise,
Nature's circus is full of surprise!

With the breeze whispering secrets so sweet,
A frog jumps in, landing right on a beet!
He croaks out a tune like a smooth crooner,
While a playful fox becomes a late bloomer.

So let us gather in this merry retreat,
Where laughter takes root and feels so complete.
In nature's embrace, all troubles can fade,
Underneath the trees, where friendships are made.

Silent Prayers in the Forest

Amidst the leaves, a whisper flows,
A rabbit kneels, in quiet repose.
He prays for snacks, for a cozy den,
While his buddy, the fox, plots mischief again.

The deer, with elegance, bobs her head,
Dreaming of carrots, from dinner spread.
While chipmunks barter for acorns galore,
In the forest market, what a wild score!

A snail in the grass calls for patience, dear,
While ants speed by, with no time for cheer.
Every creature's hoping their lunch comes first,
In this quirky communion, we laugh and we thirst.

So raise your paws, or lift up your beak,
For silent prayers that make us unique.
Together we gather, in peace and in mirth,
In the cozy embrace of our leafy hearth.

Fables Adrift in Nature

Once a cat, who fancied his style,
Sauntered through the woods, with a charming smile.
He claimed to be king, with stride oh so fine,
But slipped on a pinecone, was that a sign?

A badger then laughed, with a belly so round,
As the cat rolled over and tumbled down.
"You're not a king, you're a jester at best!"
The cat, with a wink, said, "Well, this is my jest!"

The frogs croaked tales by the shimmering creek,
Of bears that danced, and were quite unique.
With fables afloat, and humor in the air,
Each critter adds laughter, no room for despair.

So wander with joy, let the stories unfold,
In the dance of the leaves, where adventures are told.
Nature's own theater, playful and true,
Join in the fables, let laughter renew!

The Call of the Elder Tree

An elder tree beckons with branches so wide,
"Come climb up and frolic, in my foliage hide!"
A squirrel scurries, jumps around high,
While beneath a sunbeam, a cozy dog sighs.

The branches sway softly, in a comical way,
Chasing clouds as they dance, come out and play!
A ladybug spins, like a ballerina proud,
While the ants throw confetti, oh, what a crowd!

The elder tree chuckles, its bark full of glee,
As butterflies flutter, like kids at a spree.
The whispers of laughter spread light as the air,
In the heart of the forest, with joy everywhere.

So heed the call, join this whimsical scene,
Where every leaf twirls in a joyful routine.
For under this elder, let worries just cease,
In this woodland wonder, we dance with such peace.

www.ingramcontent.com/pod-product-compliance
Lightning Source LLC
Chambersburg PA
CBHW072132070526
44585CB00016B/1649